The Men of Genesis

Alda Stephens

ARPress
ILLUMINATING IDEAS.
EMPOWERING VOICES

ARPress
45 Dan Road Suite 5
Canton MA 02021

Hotline: 1(888) 821-0229
Fax: 1(508) 545-7580

Ordering Information:
Quantity sales. Special discounts are available on quantity purchases by corporations, associations, and others. For details, contact the publisher at the address above.

Printed in the United States of America.

ISBN-13: Paperback   979-8-89356-670-3
          eBook   979-8-89356-672-7
          Hardback   979-8-89356-671-0

Library of Congress Control Number: 2024904371

Prologue

Have you ever wanted to do something so much that you couldn't stand it? For most of my life, I have wanted to preach God's Word, not just convey the stories of the Bible, the prophecies of the prophets, the parables told by Christ, the death and resurrection of Christ, and the unadulterated following of Christ's disciples but to stand up for Him to those who can't bring themselves to believe in our heavenly Father who is faithful to us more than we deserve.

I've been teaching Sunday school for the last eleven years. It's been a joy to teach children God's Word. A friend of mine and fellow Sunday school teacher shared a song with me a few months back "There Was Jesus," sung by Zach Williams and Dolly Parton. I love the title and the words of the song because they pertain to you and me. Regardless of what we go through (and we've all gone through a lot this year), we are never alone. God is walking with us through the valleys of our lives as well as on the mountaintops when everything seems to be going right. Knowing this, I've wondered why so many young people are upset with a loving God. I thought of the book of Genesis. The men and women in this book had less history to fall back on, like Noah or Abraham. The faith that many had in God was genuine as it should be. Those that chose to sin against God back then perhaps never truly appreciated or understood all that He had done for them then. I believe the same could be said today.

So here I am writing a book on the men who lived in the early years of God's creation a focus on the men who withstood ridicule, taunting, favoritism, and deceit because their hearts were open to trusting and loving God. I think of Noah and all that he had to endure from those around him and the task of building a huge vessel to escape the Great Flood. I think of the 120 years that God gave the people who were sinning back then time to get their lives in order and to repent of their sins. No one came forward. Noah and his family escaped the ravenous waters. The story of Joseph toward the end of Genesis is one of my favorites because, through the difficult times he had to endure, he never lost faith in the Lord, and in the end, he forgave his brothers.

I ask this question now of you, but I could ask it of those who lived in Noah's day: who is the one with a track record of getting us through the tough spots? God was, is, and always will be the answer. Today, you and I have God's Word to prove just that. It is the truth, plain and simple. We should all be like the Apostle Paul anxiously wanting to tell others about the Gospel, about God's Word! Take the Bible and what's in it to others! In fact, run with it! Go tell your friends who live down the street from you that God exists, and His love and faithfulness is more than he or she will ever have from anyone else. We owe that to our friends and neighbors as life is fleeting, but eternity is forever.

Remember this: the Lord doesn't care if we have an iPhone 9 or 11. He is not checking off boxes as to whether today we happen to be wearing a new dress or jeans or an outfit we've had in our closet for two months! He doesn't care! What He cares about is the depth of our heart. Who or what is the Lord having to compete with in our lives? Hopefully, nothing. He wants to be on the top podium, the champion of our heart the One we believe in, the One we trust, the One we love more than anyone or anything else.

John 1:12 (HCSB) says, "But to all who did receive Him, He gave them the right to be children of God, to those who believe in His name."

As both an engineer that thrives on logic and a Sunday school teacher who truly believes in the Lord, I know having Christ in our life is the only logical path to take. In Matthew 7:24, Jesus tells the crowd, "Therefore, everyone who hears these words of mine and acts on them will be like a sensible man who built his house on the rock."

So, with all this said, I present to you the first in a series of books on the men and women of the Bible who did stand up for the Lord. In spite of all the heckling, the name-calling, and the threats on their lives, those that had faith and trust in the Lord persevered to do His will. We are at that point again today. I feel such a sadness for anyone who hasn't aligned themselves with God's Word and, for that matter, Jesus Christ.

Come to Christ!

Introduction
Genesis and the Beginning

---✝---

Have you ever been first in something? Like a spelling bee contest or in a sp orts event? Maybe you were the first one done with homework or with dinner. Well, did you know that the book of Genesis has taken first place in several categories:

- The *first* book of the Bible
- The *first* of sixty-six books contained in both the Old and New Testaments
- The *first* book of the Pentateuch
- The *first* book that introduces both God's power and His love for His people
- The *first* book in which man sinned

That gives you an idea of how important and relevant Genesis is to our lives so important that we will give Genesis a gold star for taking first place in the first four events listed above! The last one, being the "first book in which man sinned," is a sad acknowledgment, no prize there!

> What does the word history mean?
>
> a. Something that occured in the past
> b. A record, in chronological order, of important events
> c. A bundle of past events
> d. All of the above

Sometimes being first in something isn't a cause of celebration. Have you noticed that there is one thing not listed? The book of Genesis is part of the very first history book. You like history, right? Not sure? Well, what does the word *history* mean to you? Without looking at the answer, see which one in the block above meets up with your definition of history.

Believe it or not, history is a fascinating period of time. In school, you learn about the history of the United States as well as world history. You get (or should get) acquainted with people such as George Washington, Abraham Lincoln, Winston Churchill, Martin Luther King, John Kennedy and others. We learn from books and teachers about events such as the Revolutionary War, the Civil War, the Industrial Revolution, World Wars I and II, and space flights like Apollo 11's trip to the moon.

But how far back in time do your school history books take you? I have a really thick

Here are some facts of the Bible:

1. Every minute, over fifty Bibles are sold. Answer: d
2. The Bible was written over a span of 1500 years.
3. The Bible was written by over forty individuals.
4. The original language of the Old Testament was Hebrew.
5. There are sixty-six books in the Bible.
6. The Bible has 31,173 verses.
7. The shortest verse of the Bible comes from John 11:35: "Jesus Wept."

Source: Fritz, Chery. "Bible Facts." BibleReasons, www.biblereasons. com/https://biblereasons. com/bible-facts/

heavy history book on America that takes the reader back to the year 1492. Now every year is important to history some years have more happenings than others; however, we shouldn't think that the world began in 1492. Do you believe that everything began in 1492? No, of course not. There were *thousands* of years of mankind walking our earth before the likes of Christopher Columbus began discovering faraway lands. How do we know this? Well, there is a history book dating back to day 1 of this earth on which we live. What is it? None other than the Bible, God's Word.

I've always said in the Sunday school classes I've taught over the years that the Bible is the best book you will ever read. It takes you back over six thousand years ago to the earth's beginnings. When we read about the struggles they had. More importantly, we get a good understanding of the love God has for His people, including you and me. And we share in the anticipation of the second coming of our Lord Jesus Christ. And, in all this, we should give praise to God for all that He has provided us.

So, as we start at the Bible's beginning, keep this in mind from Isaiah 40:8: "The grass withers and the flowers fall, but the word of our God endures forever." We can't always say that about things in our own lives. Friends come and go. But the Bible is truthful, insightful, and its message has stayed the same throughout the years! Isn't that good to know! It describes in detail that of yesterday, that which is important for you today, and that which will determine your eternal future. (Each of us has an eternal future by the way; the choices we make in our lives will determine the location of such a future!)

You know what's really cool? The Bible is a history with one central figure whose love and concern for you and me is so great we can't even fathom the depth of such. Think about it someone who loves you and me beyond our sins. And, believe me, we are all sinners. The Apostle Paul tells us in Romans 3:23: "For all have sinned and fall short of the glory of God." Who is this loving central figure? Who is the one that has blessed us for all we have? None other than God, our heavenly Father, of course.

Have you ever tried walking in someone else's shoes? It's not easy, is it? Especially when the shoe sizes don't match. Can we walk in God's shoes? No! We are not even close to walking in God's shoes; don't ever think you can by the way! We can't do what He has done and continues to do for us. Okay, in a very, very small way, we can somewhat relate to making something from nothing, like a school project. It's not easy to do, is it? But this is what we have read and seen God doing in an enormous way. Genesis 1:1 takes us to the beginning of God's handiwork in which the earth and the heavens were created, in other words, the entire universe.

I thought of God's huge endeavor of creating the heavens and earth when we moved to a newly built home. Yes, our creations were on a much smaller scale than God's. However, our yard really needed landscaping. Now we could have just left it as is, but that would have been too boring. It needed shrubs, trees, flowers, and walkways for us to really enjoy the yard. God, in this massive universe He created, could have just been satisfied with earth as it was: formless and empty. But He desired to stamp His own imprint on earth. He must have had a lot of patience. His creative handiwork was not impulsive but carefully considered. Each day's creation was a stepping stone to the next day's development all, in the end, designed to bless mankind.

Genesis 1:2 says that "God was hovering over the surface of the waters." Can't you just see God hovering, lingering, inspecting, determining the first step that had to be made on this speck of mass that He created in the expanse of the universe. A mass known to us as earth an earth covered with water. As God hovered, He was determined to get it right. *He did.*

As we move forward not just here in Genesis but throughout the Bible, we must remember that God is all-powerful and all-knowing. He is the creator and the overseer of the universe. We are to leave it at that. Period. None of us, neither you or me, have all the answers. Sometimes, we think we do; however, many of us will search in vain to know all there is to know in the world. However, there is a limit to how much our brains are able to comprehend. As a result, we can go only so far with what we truly know. It is at this point that we need to surrender to what is stated in the Bible. It's called faith. Period. And it is this faith our belief in God that we apply at the very onset: the beginning in Genesis 1…

THE PENTATEUCH (ALSO KNOWN AS THE TORAH)

AUTHOR: GOD THROUGH MOSES

GENESIS
This is where it all began. It took six days for God to complete His creation of heaven and earth. Animals, fish, and humans would be created on days 5 and 6. On the seventh day, God would rest.

Written: Estimated to have been written in 1400 B.C.

EXODUS
The word "exodus" means "a mass departure of people, especially emigrants." In the book of Exodus we read about the Israelites exiting Egypt in 1446 BC, being led out of the country by God who uses Moses to lead His people to the promised land. The Ten Commandments are introduced in Exodus 20.

Written: The majority of the book was written between 1445 and 1405 B.C.

LEVITICUS
This book contains instructions or rules on how the Israelites were to serve God. Those that wanted a close relationship with God believed that they had to follow these rules. A part of the regulations made it possible for God to establish an earthly throne amongst His people.

Written: The book of Leviticus is thought to have been written sometime during the forty years of wandering in the wilderness.

NUMBERS
The Israelites continue to be rebellious and disobedient toward God. This book illustrates a contrast between God's continued faithfulness to and love for His people versus their continual faithlessness (rebellious, disobedience, etc.) toward God. As a result, those who were part of the exodus from Egypt did not see the Promised Land, living out their remaining years in the wilderness. Their children will, however.

Written: The book of Numbers is thought to have been written sometime during the wilderness crossing (1445 to 1405 B.C.).

DEUTERONOMY
The fifth and final book of the Pentateuch. It, like the other four, was written by God through Moses. It was meant to provide further explanation of the Law to the Israelites who were going to enter the Promised Land. These Israelites were young or not born at all at the time their parents and/or elders were sent wandering in the wilderness for forty years after disobeying God. That generation would not see the Promised Land. Moses would give three sermons to this young generation before he died: 1) The History of Israel, 2) The Law, and 3) Review of the Covenant of God.

Written: The book of Deuteronomy is thought to have been written in 1406 B.C.

Source:

Stedman, Ray. (1997). *Adventuring Through the Bible*. Discovery House Publishers.

The Week It All Started

(Reference the Creation chart on the following page as you read this section.) Let's begin by closing our eyes really tight. What do you see? Darkness, right? It's not comfortable when all we see is darkness. God, from the beginning, wanted light in our lives. So on the first day, He created light by powerfully commanding, "Let there be light." In all likelihood, it was God Himself who radiated the light on that first day. David states in Psalm 104:2 that "He wraps Himself in light as if it were a robe, spreading out the sky like a canopy."

When God gets to day 2 of His creation, we are told that He created "an expanse between the waters..." Just what is an "expanse between the waters?" The expanse, which means "something spread out," is the sky where we see all sorts of birds fly and clouds in all their forms. It is a placement for the sun, emanating light and warmth for us below, and for the moon, whether it be a half moon or full moon. On the third day, God created the dry land calling it "earth" and the water on the land "seas."

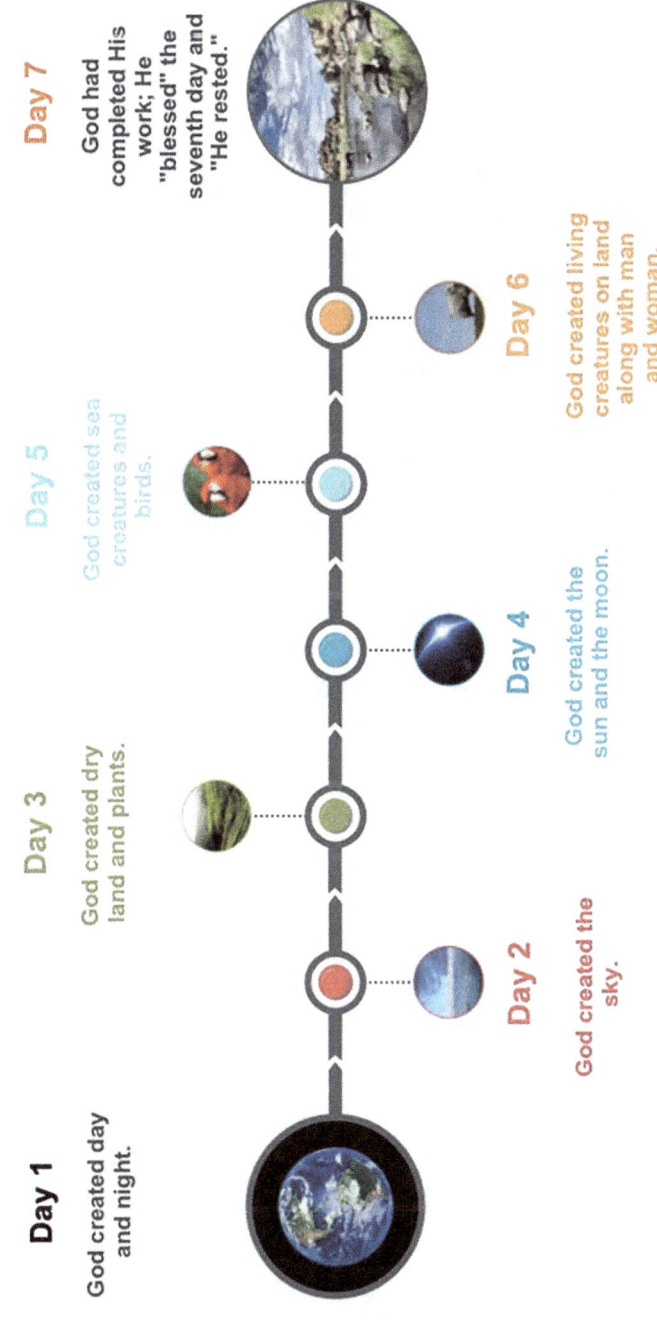

Creation
Genesis 1:1-2:3

Day 1

God created day and night.

Day 2

God created the sky.

Day 3

God created dry land and plants.

Day 4

God created the sun and the moon.

Day 5

God created sea creatures and birds.

Day 6

God created living creatures on land along with man and woman.

Day 7

God had completed His work; He "blessed" the seventh day and "He rested."

Have you ever looked at stars from the top of a mountain? You feel that much closer to them; every star is that much more vivid, right? It's almost like you could reach out and grab one. It's even more amazing to look through a telescope at the stars, the planets, and the moon. If you have ever done so, you recognize not just how awesome the sight is of each but also the amazing workmanship of God.

The day and night that He provided for us on the first day would, on the fourth day, be further defined with a sun that provides us brightness and warmth during the day, stars to guide us, and the moon's light to navigate by in the darkness of the night. The light coming from these three would form both our days (the hours) and years ahead.

God would gift us the beautiful creatures of the water and air. Such creatures are a joy to see. If you and your family have been to Alaska, you've probably seen the orca or humpback whales. All of this plus more in the seas and the many species of birds in the sky are God's masterpieces He created on the fifth day. They all have a purpose in God's creation just like you do. On the sixth day, God would not only create living creatures that would roam the land livestock or farm animals, crawling creatures such as bugs, and wildlife like deer, bear, tigers, and elephants but also (drum roll please) *mankind!* Open your Bible and read Genesis 1:26: "God said, 'Let Us make man in Our image, according to Our likeness.'"

What Sets Mankind (You and Me) Apart from God's Other Creations?

Let's think about this for a moment. This question doesn't just deal with the physical characteristics but the inner soul. Oh yes, we each have our own characteristics. Compared to me and others, you have your own uniqueness in your appearance, personality, and what you value. But have you wondered just what is meant by the word *soul?* Well, it's a deep emotional thing. Yours and my soul are made up of what we think about things presented to us, how we feel, our willingness to follow, and what we perceive. Erwin Raphael McManus in his book *Soul Cravings,* says that his soul "always desires and demands." Since we are made in the image of God, desiring more, however, will never truly be met by material stuff. God created mankind to have a relationship with us. So when you peel away the layers of who we are, the core need is to have a loving relationship with God, seeking to do His will. Period. No other entity created by God has this innate desire.

The global financial services bank, Capital One, many times has its commercials end with, "What's in your wallet?" God is always saying, "What's in your heart?" And it is this question that determines where you are in the following four areas areas possessed by humans only, areas driven by your heart and soul, areas that were on display by the men of Genesis. After reading this book, assess not only how important these four areas were to the men of Genesis but how important they are in your life as well.

1. *Your moral life.* Okay, this one is very important. The *Oxford Dictionary* defines moral as being "concerned with the principles of right and wrong behavior and the goodness or badness of human character." God has given you the ability to discern the difference between right and wrong. However, man has had an ongoing bout with this issue for a very long time, in fact, back to the days of Adam and Eve. You might think, *What's the big deal?* The big deal is that your character is a driver of your future. Maybe you feel justified with your demeanor "I'm not hurting anyone." Well, your character sets the wheels in motion, so to speak. It is on display for all to see. It speaks volumes in today's society in which certain morals are losing their importance. You will read in the next chapter about Noah's task after the people's lack of morals made God angry.

2. *To be Spiritual or non-spiritual.* For Christians, spirituality is defined as displaying or practicing that of the Christian faith. It means our "new" lives reflect that of Christ we are more like Him in how we live our lives. Isn't it exciting to know that you and I have been restored favorably with God because when all is said and done, we need to have a relationship with Him. Christ came to earth to die for our sins. He rose on the third day and sit at the right hand of God the Father. When we

accept that as truth, we are a "new" creation. We live a better life in accordance to God's will for us. Second Corinthians 5:17 tells us, "Therefore, if anyone is in Christ, he is a new creation; old things have passed away, and look, new things have come." As a result of this spirituality we have, we can communicate with the Lord. In the Old Testament, Noah, Abraham, Isaac, and Jacob each had personal encounters with the Lord. Joseph's encounters with God would come in the form of dreams.

3. *Your ability to rationalize.* Man's ability to think sets him apart from the other living creatures, right? You and I are able to apply reason and logic to situations we find ourselves in or may find ourselves in thereby planning ahead where necessary. For instance, we reason that if our grade point average (GPA) is close to or at 4.0 and we have a high SAT score, we can get into any Ivy League university. Logic tells you to wear a coat outside when it's cold or to not put a hand out to a strange dog. Noah, wanting to know if there was any dry land showing after the flood, first sent out a raven then a dove. Both came back as there wasn't any dry land on which they could land. It wasn't until the dove was sent out on its third journey that it didn't return it found land! Noah showed reason in doing such. Joseph, correctly interpreting the dreams of Pharaoh, was able to not only save the people of Egypt during the famine but also his family.

4. *Relational/Dependence.* God sought to have a relationship with mankind from the very beginning. He seeks the same with you and me today. Think about this. Here He is all-knowing, all-powerful, and everywhere. Why would He need anyone else? He could have propped His feet up and said, *I'm good here by myself.* But He didn't. He wanted that relationship with mankind. And it has shown for over six thousand years through His provisions and His love for us. We need to remember that each of us has been created for a purpose. Knowing this, we should embrace Him desiring to do His will.

On the seventh day of God's creation, viewing all that He brought about, He was pleased. You can imagine God with a checklist checking off all the necessities He knew mankind needed to survive, the ultimate one being a relationship with God Himself. And so on the seventh day, He rested.

The evidence we have around us points to God's mighty hand in earth's creation and mankind. There is no doubt about God's role in all we see and who we are. As my husband and I took a boat ride down the Colorado River last year, rising up on either side of us were thousands of feet of canyon walls. The river trip took us around Horseshoe Bend, considered to be part of the "east rim of the Grand Canyon." As our eyes scaled the cliffs in all directions, we could see fossil bearing sedimentary layers stacked on top of each other. I thought about the

Here are what I consider to be the top ten morals on which we need to or should base our lives on:

- First and foremost, treat others as you want to be treated (the Golden Rule, Matthew 7:12).
- *Take responsibility* for your actions.
- Do respect others.
- Have the courage to do what is right (we are told in Romans 12:2, "Do not be conformed to this world…").
- Forgive as you too seek forgiveness (the Lord's Prayer).
- Work hard at your job, both inside and outside your home.
- Be honest; lying is never the answer.
- Be a team player; cooperate with other people.
- Make adjustments as life is not all about us (JOY Jesus first, Others second, You last).
- Do not take what isn't yours.

evolutionists and their theories. All my husband and I could think of was the impact from the rising surging waters of the Great Flood. Bodie Hodge authored a book, *Tower of Babel*, in which he summarizes the Bible's response this way to those doubters: "Being image-bearers of God distinguishes us from animals and shows the value that God has in mankind. God became a man, not an animal. Christ came to save mankind (that is, sinners), not to save animals. He came to die in the place of descendants of Adam and Eve, or Adam's race."

So I ask the question, how do we look at history associated with Genesis 2 and beyond, let alone the history of America thousands of years later, for instance, without acknowledging what God did for us in Genesis 1? Those who question Genesis 1 are not able, through any evidence, to prove that the earth has been around longer than just over six thousand years, that such a "big bang" occurred. For Christians, the starting point is Genesis 1:1…

Noah and the Great Flood
Choice Between Right and Wrong

✛

Do you know that when you were just nineteen months old, you knew the difference between right and wrong? You knew it! That's pretty cool! Did you also know that you, as children, make up to three thousand decisions a day! Wow, that's a lot! Well, we, humans, have been making choices since the days following God's creation of heaven and earth. Some choices have been weird so much so that you want to ask like, "Why, Adam and Eve, did you do that?" Adam and Eve had a *perfect* life in the Garden of Eden until Eve made the choice (and Adam agreed with her) to eat from the tree of the knowledge of good and evil. They had other trees to eat from, but they accepted the serpent's word over that of God's. There were consequences for their disobedience including having to leave the Garden of Eden. Or what about Lot (Abraham's nephew)? Lot and his family were *rescued* from the evil that was going on in Sodom and Gomorrah; however, Lot's wife decided to look back at the destruction of Sodom and Gomorrah after the angels of the Lord earlier warned, "Don't look back, and don't stop anywhere on the plain." She was turned into a pillar of salt.

Listen to and Obey the Lord!

In Exodus 12, God, through Moses, *brought the Israelites out of slavery,* out of the land of Egypt, to the Promised Land. The Israelites were free! Praise the Lord! Yet in Exodus 32, we read that Aaron used the gold that the Israelites had accumulated to make a golden calf to worship as their god and then allowed the people to celebrate in accordance with their own desires. What in the world! This was totally wrong! Making an idol of anything and worshiping it was a rebellious act resulting in God's judgment. God was not happy! In fact, He was angry. There would be a day of reckoning for their sinful actions. Many times, when we sin, we don't think it's that big a deal. However, it is wrong to think that way. What someone thinks as "not a big deal" in committing a sin can have impacts on others. And eventually, there will be accountability to God!

Okay, so on the bright side, other choices made by mankind in obedience to the Lord result in blessings bestowed upon them by the Lord. One such instance in the Bible invovled Noah. When we hear the name Noah, most of us immediately equate the name with the person who built the Ark to deal wtih the impending Flood. While that's important, we should keep in mind that it was his faith in the Lord that underscored his obedience in constructing the Ark. Faith is what got Noah up in the morning, got him through the heat of the day with the sun

Conformity with today's culture below are a few good points made by John Stonestreet and Brett Kunkle in their book, *A Practical Guide to Culture:*

- "We're to be disciples who make other disciples."
- "Many Germans, including Christians, chose to remain silent and do nothing to resist Hitler and the Nazi regime."
- "We need to courageously navigate the threatening currentsknowing that we serve a cause, and a God, far greater than ourselves."

beating down on him, and at night with an aching body, faith was the assurance that what he was doing was right.

During this period of time, we're told in Genesis 6:9 that "Noah walked with God." Through his obedience, Noah was seen favorably by God. In the early years of God's creation, we see a man who chose not to be coerced into an immoral life but rather chose to follow the Lord. He did not feel he had to be like everyone else. Do you feel like you need to be like everyone else to fit in? Don't believe that! The only one you need to please is God. Although written thousands of years later, Noah followed the Apostle Paul's edict of Romans 12:2: "Do not be conformed to this age, but be transformed by the renewing of your mind, so that you may discern what is the good, pleasing, and perfect will of God." At the end of the day, there is only one voice we should listen to, and that is God's voice. Noah did just that. He is mentioned in nine books of the Bible, five of which are in the New Testament. Following God's will, Noah would take on a monstrous endeavor of constructing a nearly five-hundred-foot long vessel that would save both he and his family along with hundreds of species of animals. Behind his back were villagers laughing and jeering at him thinking he was being ridiculous taking on such an undertaking.

Sin and Consequences

There were over sixteen hundred years of existence from the time of Adam to when the Flood occurred. In between the fall of Adam and Eve and the earth being covered with water, sin maneuvered its way further into the minds and deeds of many living on earth. After the Fall, one such example was Cain killing his brother Abel, jealous of the relationship Abel had with the Lord. The Tenth Commandment tells us we are not to covet what others have. God knows our needs. Sometimes, our wants are not our needs. God also knows our hearts. I believe Cain's heart was wicked. In the case of Cain murdering his brother, the Lord punished him accordingly.

The generations that would follow Adam and Eve were ungodly. It is unknown as to how much Adam and Eve taught their children of the Lord. Cain's act, along with that of his descendant Lamech, point out the self-serving traits of man. Even back then, it was all about one's self. The sinful nature of man not only disappointed the Lord but resulted in His decision to do away with mankind. Warren Wiersbe states that "God is long-suffering with lost sinners, but there comes a time when judgment must fall," and it did on all but one family. At that time, water covered the whole earth. Through God's grace, Noah and his family were spared along with two of each animal that existed on the earth.

Noah

So who was Noah? The Bible tells us that he was the son of another man named Lamech whose father was Methuselah. Methuselah was a descendant of Seth, Adam and Eve's third son. The Bible tells us that "Adam was 130 years old when he fathered a son in his likeness according to his image…" (Genesis 5:3). Seth's great-great-great-great grandson Methuselah lived to be 969 years old (Genesis 5:27). He is considered to be the oldest living being in the Bible. Believing he was a loving grandfather, I would like to think he may have helped his grandson, Noah, build the Ark prior to his passing.

Why the name Noah? Many times, a child's name has special meaning. In the case of Noah, we are told in Genesis 5:29 that Lamech picked the name Noah because "this one will bring us relief from the agonizing labor of our hands caused by the ground the *Lord* has cursed." *The The Matthew Henry Commentary* points out that the name Noah means "rest," which is what Noah was able to do following 120 years of preparation for the building of the Ark and another 377 days of enduring the waters of the Flood and subsequent receding of such waters. Thousands of years later, the Apostle Peter stated in 2 Peter 2:5 that Noah was "a preacher of righteousness."

TIMELINE TO NOAH
INFOGRAPHIC

"Yes, Christianity is about Jesus, and moral and spiritual truths - and relationships. But the truth concerning these is founded in real history - on God's Word beginning in Genesis."

Ken Ham
Founder and CEO
Answers in Genesis

7 Days

God's Creation

God would, in six days, create:
Day 1 - Light
Day 2 - Sky
Day 3 - Dry Land and Vegetation
Day 4 - Sun, moon, and stars
Day 5 - Living creatures in the water and birds
Day 6 - Living creatures on the land including man and woman
Day 7 - Rest

Sin is introduced into the world.

Adam and Eve

After the Fall, Adam and Eve would start a family. Their first child was a son named Cain. Their second child was also a son whom they named Abel. Following the death of Abel, they would have another son, Seth. Adam was 130 years old when Seth was born. Adam lived to be 930 years old.

Mankind continues its immoral ways.

Sin continues with rebellion and murder.

Cain and Abel

Genesis 4:2 tells us that "Abel became a shepherd of flocks, but Cain worked the ground." Both men provided offerings to the Lord; however, the Lord could tell Cain's heart was not in his offerings. The Lord had high regards for Abel's offering - "some of the firstborn of his flock and their fat portions." (Genesis 4:4) Being jealous and angry, Cain killed Abel - the first instance since God's Creation that a man's blood was shed.

Cain vs. Abel

Sin Amongst Men

Man would continue to fall.

120 years before the Flood, God tells Noah that "I have decided to put an end to every creature, for the earth is filled with wickedness because of them."

Noah and the Flood

Noah trusted God. He and his family entered the Ark along with the animals that God told him to bring onto the Ark. After 377 days, the land was dry allowing Noah and the others to exit the Ark. God would make a covenant with Noah that He would never destroy every living thing on the earth again. Hence, the rainbow - God's sign of His forever faithfulness.

Faithfulness

From the article, "Faith and Creation," - It [creation] was intentionally brought into existence by God who knew the end from the beginning and designed all things well."

25

120 Years The Extended Warning

Jude 14–15 says, "And Enoch, in the seventh generation from Adam, prophesied about them: 'Look! The Lord comes with thousands of His holy ones to execute judgment on all and to convict them of all their ungodly acts that they have done in an ungodly way, and of all the harsh things ungodly sinners have said against Him.'"

The Lord was saddened with how mankind had turned out. There was so much wickedness occurring on earth. The level to which society had sunk was alarming. The evils of the people were drowning out all that the Lord had provided for them. Any and all sin is an offense to God. In Genesis 6:3, the Lord set a time limit as to how much longer such immorality would exist, putting the deadline for such atrocities at 120 years. The people had time 120 years to change their evil ways. Ken Ham, in his book *The New Answers Book 4*, states that God was not setting man's lifespan at 120 years. He was merely giving Noah a well-in-advanced warning of what was to come and when. It was a grace period for man to repent of his sins. However, like many today, they would not obey the Lord. Paul Taylor, in his article, "Noah the Evangelist," put it this way: "When the door to the Ark was shut, there was room for many more people. All they had to do was repent and turn to God. *That's all any of us have to do today; if you haven't done so, ask the Lord for forgiveness of your sins, and put your faith in Him.*

Genesis 6:8 tells us that "Noah, however, found favor in the sight of the *Lord.*" God would spend time walking with Noah. Wouldn't that be awesome to have a daily walk with God conversing about the ways of the people! What made Noah so special? Noah was a man of integrity. He believed in and trusted the Lord, obeying His commands. Throughout the Bible, we read of obedience being exhibited on the part of the Lord's followers in spite of possible persecution. We all should be disciples for the Lord. In the Old Testament, there were not only the prophets but also others like Rahab, Esther, Moses, Joshua, Deborah, and David who would risk their lives for God. In the New Testament, there were the apostles. For instance, after Jesus's ascension into heaven, Peter and the other apostles found themselves in trouble before the Sanhedrin for performing miracles. Peter defended their actions by saying, "We must obey God rather than men" (see Acts 5:29). John MacArthur writes this about obedience in his book *The Gospel According to Paul*: "Although our own good works, obedience, and holy living are not in any way the ground of our justification, they are nevertheless inevitable fruits of genuine faith…" If we truly have faith in the Lord, we will not only desire to obey Him, we will do as He commands us to!

The Great Flood

At the end of the 120 years of preparation following God's decision to put an end to all but a designated number of living creatures on earth, the time had come for Noah, his family, and two of each animal, male and female, to step inside the Ark. God gave Noah seven days to get everyone on board the Ark. Some consider this an additional seven days of grace for those sinning against God to repent. No one did.

The Ark was massive in size! Using modern day measurement of a cubit being 20.4 inches, the ark was

Five-hundred-ten feet long (300 cubits long), it was 1–1/2 times the length of a football field which is 360 feet in total length.

Eighty-five feet wide (50 cubits wide), about half the width of a football field, which is 160 feet wide.

Fifty-one feet high (30 cubits high), about 1/25 as tall as the Empire State Building (1250 feet tall) but tall enough to accommodate three decks inside.

Noah had built the Ark to God's specifications. Can you imagine being Noah? He had heard all the jeering, the taunting, the laughing at him for all these years from those who had turned their backs on the Lord. He and his family along with the animals were now going to step inside a vessel designed by the Lord that would save their lives from a monumental flood that would take the lives of those on earth whose wickedness had consumed them instead of the Lord's love. There was no hesitation on the part of Noah, no looking back. After Noah's family and all the animals got on board, the door to the Ark closed.

We read in Genesis 7:11 that the Flood began on the seventeenth day of the second month. Noah was, at that time, six hundred years old! Tightly secured in the Ark, he and his family no doubt heard the skies open and the deluge of rain pouring down onto the wooden boat. The rain would continue for forty days and forty nights.

> The flood continued for 40 days on the earth; the waters increased and lifted up the ark so that it rose above the earth. The waters surged and increased greatly on the earth, and the ark floated on the surface of the water. Then the waters surged even higher on the earth, and all the high mountains under the whole sky were covered. The mountains were covered as the waters surged above them more than 20 feet. Every creature perished those that crawl on the ear, birds, livestock, wildlife, and those that swarm on the earth, as well as all mankind. (Genesis 7:17–21)

After the rain had stopped, powerful waters continued to rise above the earth for another 110 days.

The Waters Go Away

Following the surge of water across the earth, over the next 150 days, the waters would slowly recede. God would use a powerful wind to begin drying up the water. The sources of the rain "were closed." During this time, the Ark would end up on "the mountains of Ararat." This mountainous region is located in today's Turkey.

It wasn't until seventy-four days later that mountaintops on the earth became visible. Patiently waiting another forty days, Noah would send out a raven through an opened window of the Ark followed seven days later by a dove. There were no signs of dry land. It wasn't until another seven days had passed that Noah would send the dove out again. This time, the dove would return with an olive leaf in her beak finally a sign for Noah that the waters had gone down. Waiting another seven days, Noah would send the dove out again. It did not return. On the first day of the first month of the new year, Noah would remove the covering (some believe this was a window or a hatch) from the Ark. He saw the land was drying. Fifty-seven days later, the earth was dry.

Instead of rushing to the door, Noah's faith in the Lord and his desire to obey meant he would have to wait for God's command to exit the Ark. In Genesis 8:15–19, we read that God gave Noah the go ahead to go outside along with his family and all the animals. You can imagine how grateful Noah was to God when exiting the Ark. When he stepped off the Ark, Noah built an altar to the Lord. On the altar, he also offered some of the clean animals as burnt offerings to the Lord. In response to this worship, God made a covenant with Noah that He would "never again curse the ground because of man, even though man's inclination is evil from his youth. And I will never again strike down every living thing as I have done."

> "He said, 'Even more, those who hear the word of God and keep it are blessed'" (Luke 11:28).

Covenant and the Rainbow

What exactly is a covenant? *Merriam-Webster Dictionary* defines *covenant* as "a usually formal, solemn, and binding agreement." Following the flood, God would make a covenant with Noah and all living creatures on earth. In Genesis 9: 9–11, God states the following to Noah:

> Understand that I am confirming My covenant with you and your descendants after you, and with every living creature that is with you birds, livestock, and all wildlife of the earth that are with you all the animals of the earth that came out of the ark. I confirm My covenant with you that never again will every creature

be wiped out by the waters of a flood; there will never again be a flood to destroy the earth.

Keep this in mind: when God makes a covenant with man, it is a very serious binding agreement that He has put together. His commitment to His creation should never be doubted; His faithfulness to man has been and always will be assured because of His love for us. And this is so telling in the covenant with Noah. A sign of this covenant is the rainbow. God tells us in Genesis 9:13–15: "I have placed My bow in the clouds, and it will be a sign of the covenant between Me and the earth. Whenever I form clouds over the earth and the bow appears on the clouds, I will remember My covenant between Me and you and all the living creatures: water will never again become a flood to destroy every creature."

Abraham - The First Great Patriarch

While each person's faith journey is unique, Abraham blazed a trail for the rest of us; his faith journey tells us about our own.
— Charles R. Swindoll, pastor and author of *Abraham*

After the Great Flood, the land would begin to populate again. And its people with its immoralities would begin to mirror that which existed before the Great Flood. Bodie Hodge, in his book *Tower of Babel*, points out that "the descendants of Noah started to look for other things to worship." The Flood would not put an end to the rebelliousness against God that Adam and Eve started over seventeen hundred years earlier.

Following the Great Flood, Noah's sons, Shem, Ham, and Japheth, would have families that would eventually spread out across many nations including the Middle East, today's northern part of Africa, (i.e., Egypt) and Asia. As we follow their movement, keep in mind the curse that Noah put on Ham and his descendants. Due to Ham's actions against his father, following the Great Flood, Noah would curse Ham's son, Canaan, making him a slave to Ham's brothers, Shem and Japheth.

The Sons and Grandsons of Noah and the Land They Founded

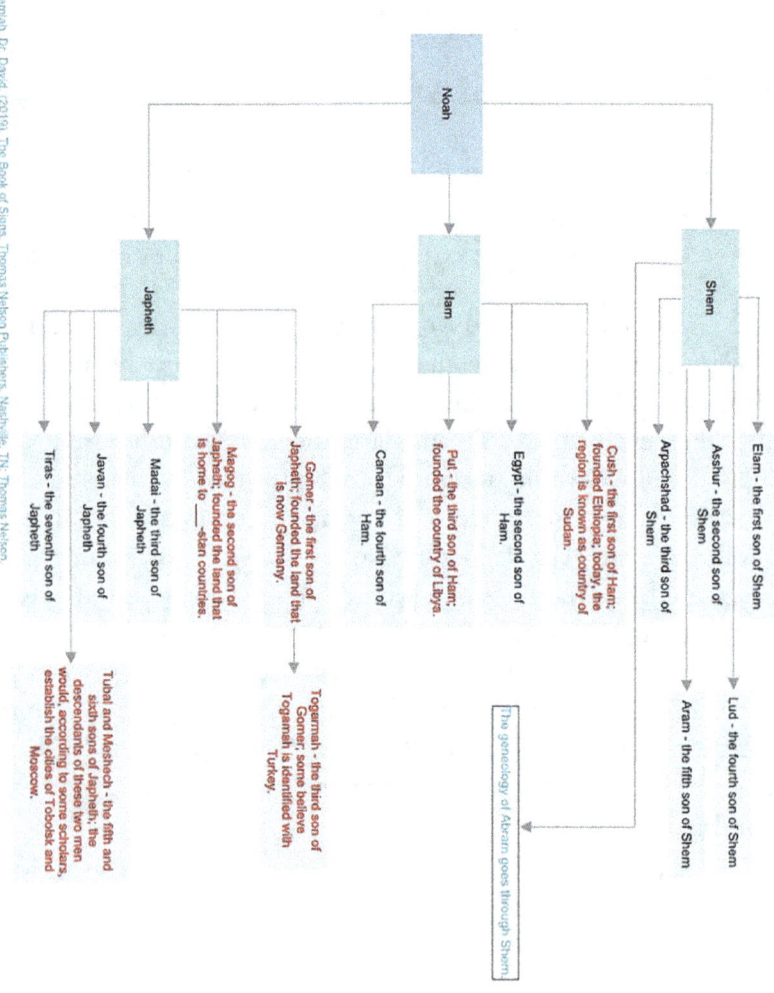

Source: Jeremiah, Dr. David. (2019). The Book of Signs. Thomas Nelson Publishers, Nashville, TN: Thomas Nelson.

Noah

Japheth

Ham

Shem

Tiras - the seventh son of Japheth

Javan - the fourth son of Japheth

Madai - the third son of Japheth

Magog - the second son of Japheth; founded the land that is home to ___ -stan countries.

Gomer - the first son of Japheth; founded the land that is now Germany.

Canaan - the fourth son of Ham.

Put - the third son of Ham; founded the country of Libya.

Egypt - the second son of Ham.

Cush - the first son of Ham; founded Ethiopie; today, the region is known as country of Sudan.

Arpacnshad - the third son of Shem

Asshur - the second son of Shem

Elam - the first son of Shem

Lud - the fourth son of Shem

Aram - the fifth son of Shem

The genealogy of Abram goes through Shem.

Tubal and Meshech - the fifth and sixth sons of Japheth; the descendants of these two men would, according to some scholars, establish the cities of Tobolsk and Moscow.

Togarmah - the third son of Gomer; some believe Togarmah is identified with Turkey.

The Tower of Babel - Here We Go Again

We are told in Genesis 10:8 that Cush, Ham's son, fathered Nimrod who became "the most powerful man on earth." It is not known as to whether the generations that followed Noah were made aware of the reasons behind the Great Flood or, for that matter, the truth about the one God who created earth, its properties, and mankind. Regardless, mankind will always be made up of those who believe they are better than God. Such was the case with Nimrod who would go to the land of Shinar (the country with two rivers Tigris and Euphrates, a reference to Babylonia). While in the land of Shinar, Nimrod and others would start constructing the Tower of Babel. Their actions were a rebellious act toward God who had told the people to not just multiply but to scatter across the face of the earth as well. As it so often occurs with leaders, control was Nimrod's thing. He apparently wanted all the people under him. But why a tower? There have been many theories. Hodge listed these in his book:

> *They were afraid of another catastrophe like the Global Flood.* Were their hearts so far removed from God that the covenant God made with Noah had little to no significance?
>
> *These people were really into worshipping all sorts of gods.* So maybe these people, distancing themselves even further from God, were into idolatry, building a temple in reverence to a false god.
>
> *Everyone wants fame.* Another word for fame is pride. They were very proud people, so perhaps they wanted to take credit for something instead of giving it to God. Proverbs 16:18 tells us, "Pride goes before destruction, and a haughty spirit before a fall."
>
> *There were suggestions that the people were stargazers.* Descendants of Noah worshipped the stars including Abram's father, Terah, who worshipped the "moon god."

In all likelihood, the people started building for fame. They wanted the accolades, not God. They wanted to be in control of their destiny, not God. However, God knew what was going on. Being all-knowing and all-powerful, God did not tolerate the arrogance shown in constructing this tower. Why should He? Genesis 11:5 tells us that He came down and saw the rebellious act of the people. As a consequence for their actions, He did two things: (1) He gave them different languages and then (2) scattered the people across several lands. Today, there are over 6,500 languages spoken across the world.

God Chooses Abraham

(Note: We will refer to Abraham, at this time, as Abram. This is the name he was given at birth and was called for the majority of his life.)

Shem was the middle son of Noah, born sometime around 2448 BC. He and his older brother, Japheth, were favored by Noah. It is important to note that Shem's role and importance go beyond being the middle child. First and foremost, the genealogy of Shem includes Abram and Jesus Christ.

Second, Shem would father the Semitic people which included the Jewish people. Shem's descendants, the Israelites, would eventually do two important things: acquire the Promised Land and, in doing so, would overtake the Canaanites who were descendants of Ham.

Abram's story begins in Genesis 11. Abram's father was Terah who lived 205 years. There were seven generations between Shem and Terah. Abram had two brothers, Nahor and Haran. Haran was the father of Lot. Haran would die leaving Terah to take care of his grandson, Lot. There isn't any mention in this chapter of Genesis as to how Haran died. Abram would play a big role in the life of his nephew Lot.

At God's command to leave his birth country, Abram and his wife, Sarai, along with Lot would travel with Terah from Ur to what they thought would be their ultimate destination the land of Canaan. The trip would have covered nearly two thousand miles! Instead, Abram and his family would end up in Haran, approximately six hundred miles from Ur. There they would settle.

Did it matter to Abram that they would curtail their travels by more than one thousand miles? We will see that it mattered to God. Would Haran end up being Abram's final stomping ground? No. However, Terah would die in Haran at the age of 205.

The Abrahamic Covenant

Abram had found favor with the Lord. As Chuck Swindoll points out in his book *Abraham*, such favor wasn't a result of anything magnificent Abram did. After all, like his father and others, Abram worshipped idols. Ancient Mesopotamia was known for its reverence of mythical gods. However, as seen throughout the Bible, God chooses the weakest to be in His company. One needs to look no further than Saul of Tarsus whom the Lord would use immensely for the proclamation of the Gospel. The Apostle Paul states in 1 Corinthians 1:27, "Instead, God has chosen what is foolish in the world to shame the wise, and God has chosen what is weak in the world to shame the strong."

In Genesis 12, we are reacquainted with faithfulness and trust. In the previous chapter of this book, we read about the trust Noah had in God as he built the massive ark that would house him and his family along with animals as the earth was covered with water. God was faithful to Noah. With Abram, he too uprooted his family in accordance with God's will. Like Noah, we will see the utmost faith Abram had in God. Throughout the Bible, we see God's faithfulness to His people; *we are to be faithful to Him.*

Genesis 12:1–3 addresses the covenant God makes with Abram the Abrahamic Covenant. Unlike the Noahic Covenant, there were conditions to be met in order for Abram to receive the blessings of the Lord. Abram had to pack up all his and his family's belongings and travel on to the land of Canaan from Ur (his birthplace) in accordance with God's directive.

"The *Lord* said to Abram: Go out from your land, your relatives, and your father's house to the land that I will show you" (Genesis 12:1).

Imagine having to move from a place of comfort, a place where you have become established to travel thousands of miles to what God is promising to be a new "land." But this is what having trust in God means! In a devotional, *Next Level Leadership*, the author points out that "you inevitably will face situations where you can make a difference if you have the courage and conviction to do so." Abram had that courage and conviction and foremost, *trust*!

"he said,

'Canaan will be cursed. He will be the lowest of slaves to his brothers'"

(Genesis 9:25).

As part of the covenant established with Abram, God said in Genesis 12:2–3: "I will make you into a great nation, I will bless you, I will make your name great, and you will be a blessing. I will bless those who bless you, I will curse those who treat you with contempt, and all the peoples on earth will be blessed through you."

In verses 2 and 3 of Genesis 12, the words *bless* and *blessing* are used five times. What is God telling Abram in the midst of this upheaval when He says, "I will bless you?" Go to Matthew 5:3–12; here, you will see Jesus use the word *blessed* several times while preaching the Beatitudes during the Sermon on the Mount. Jesus' use of the word *blessed* comes from the Greek word *makarios* which means (according to Bible Study Tools) "happy." Jesus is telling His listeners, *Hey, congratulations for you have found favor with God*. In the beginning of Genesis 12, God is telling Abram that going forward, He has Abram's welfare taken care of, that he has found favor with God. That had to be a good feeling. A commentary in the *HCSB Study Bible for Women* puts it this way:

"He must leave a land to receive a land. He must leave relatives in order to become part of a great nation. He must leave his close family so that all the peoples on earth might become his family."

To want to do His will shows Him that you love the Lord with all your heart and that you believe in Him totally. Proverbs 3:5 tells us to "trust in the *Lord* with all your heart, and do not rely on your own understanding." Jesus tells a crowd in Luke 14:26, "If anyone comes to

Me and does not hate his own father and mother, wife and children, brothers and sisters yes, and even his own life he cannot be My disciple." Jesus was not saying to disobey one's parents. He was saying that you must be willing to give up everything to follow Him, the Lord. In the case of Abram, he didn't necessarily do that for the Lord.

Genesis 11:31 tells us Abram had obeyed God somewhat. Abram was supposed to leave his family behind when he left Ur. However, "He took his wife Sarai, his nephew Lot, all the possessions they had accumulated, and the people he had acquired in Haran, and set out for the land of Canaan."

Swindoll tells us God knew before Abram and his family left that taking his family would end up being a distraction to Abram. And it was. If only mankind would listen to God, but we think we know better! Wrong!

Abram and his family along with his servants would travel on the land of Canaan. Abram built an altar to the Lord in Shechem at the oak of Moreh after the Lord tells Abram that the land on which he was standing will be given "to your offspring." Imagine being told that! God is good!

By the way the "oak of Moreh" is considered to have much history. Greg Cumming, in his article "The Terebinth Tree of Moreh," points out that the tree would have been great in size at the same time of Abram building the altar and whose growth probably began after the Great Flood occurred about 350 years beforehand.

Discuss below how Abram disobeyed god

_____

_____

_____

_____

_____

_____

The meaning of building an altar: Bible Study Tools defines altars as "places where the divine and human worlds interacted. God responded actively to altar activity." Living Stream Ministry states this about the significance of an altar. "Building an altar means that we offer everything we are and have to God... The real worship of the called ones is to put all that we are and have on the altar."

According to Cumming, it would later be a landmark for the following occurrences:

> The confiscation of "foreign gods and their earrings," which Jacob would hide under the oak near Shechem (Genesis 35:4).
>
> Jacob's sons would herd their father's flocks close to the landmark of Abram's altar to the *Lord* (Genesis 37:12).
>
> Following the people's commitment to God, "We will worship the *Lord* our God and obey Him" (Joshua 24:24). Joshua would make "a covenant" for the people at Shechem and established a statute and ordinance for them. Joshua recorded these things in the book of the law of God; he also took a large stone and set it up there under the oak next to the sanctuary of the *Lord* (Joshua 24:25–26).

Traveling further south, Abram would build an altar to the *Lord* located east of Bethel. That area is known today as Jerusalem. He would then call on Yahweh.

Onto Egypt

A famine would strike the land. A famine occurs where there is a shortage or scarcity of food. Canaan was so dependent on rain to water the crops, thus famines were a regular occurrence there. At the time of Abram, Genesis 12:10 tells us that the famine was "severe." Knowing this, Abram took his family and his herd down into Egypt. He would be leaving the Promised Land. Did Abram, who had shown faith in God since leaving his birth country, pray to God asking for His guidance as to what he should do because of the famine? Did Abram seek God's counsel as to what he needed to do? No, he didn't. Swindoll said Abram "became an expert" on what he needed to do instead of relying on God.

Remember in Genesis 12:1, God told Abram that he was to leave all that he had his land, his relatives, and his father's house. That was a big deal! We will see one of the reasons why…

Genesis 12:11 tells us that as Abram and his family got close to entering Egypt, Abram became concerned about their safety and well-being. His wife, Sarai, was a beautiful woman. His concern was that someone would take his wife and kill him. So Abram would devise a plan telling his wife to "please say you're my sister so it will go well for me because of you, and my life will be spared on your account" (Genesis 12:13). In reality, she was his half sister. So Abram wasn't being totally truthful. He leaves the land of Canaan, the Promised Land, without seeking God's permission or instructions on what to do, and now he lies about his wife. Nevertheless, Sarai would submit to Abram.

As they travel into Egypt, it happened as Abram had worried about. The Egyptians saw how beautiful Sarai was. Pharaoh was told about her, and soon thereafter, she was taken into Pharaoh's home. Abram was treated well but worried about Sarai. God would intervene showing His faithfulness to Abram, a man who, as of late, was not faithful to God. God would protect Sarai where Abram failed to do so.

Plagues brought forth by God on Pharaoh and his household because of Sarai's situation caused Pharaoh to become angry with Abram. He wondered why Abram lied about Sarai being his sister. He told Abram to leave with Sarai and all his belongings, including that which he gave Abram. Abram would go back as a wealthy man.

Whatever became of Lot, Abram's nephew? Well, after Abram's journey to Egypt, he would head back to the land between Bethel and Ai to the area in which he first pitched his tent (see Genesis 12:8). Upon doing so, Abram would build an altar to the *Lord*. He would call on Yahweh at that time.

Shortly thereafter, Abram and Lot would determine that the land they were both using for their flocks and tents weren't enough to support both of their groups. There was bickering between the two groups. Abram approached Lot, telling him, "Please, let's not have quarreling between you and me, or between your herdsmen and my herdsmen, since we are relatives" (Genesis 13:8). It was necessary for the men and their families to separate.

Although Abram would have been in his right to have first choice of the section of land on which to live, he graciously let Lot choose first. "Separate from me: if you go to the left, I will go to the right; if you go to the right, I will go to the left" (Genesis 13:9). Have you made a decision after praying to God trusting Him that He would provide? Abram trusted God knowing that He would provide for him and his family. So Lot, in his state of greed, took the land that looked the most green, the most lush the Jordan Valley. Abram would move and "live near the oaks of Mamre at Hebron" (Genesis 13:18). He would then build an altar to the *Lord*.

Lot and Abram had shared land with Bethel (means "house of God") as its center. Lot's center was now Sodom.

The Impact of Decisions

The impact decisions have on our future…

Looks can be deceiving. Lot would learn the hard way. Following the battles between nine kings, Lot would be taken captive by the following four kings:

Chedorlaomer, king of Elam
Tidal, king of Goyim
Amraphel, king of Shinar
Arioch, king of Ellasar

Genesis 14:11 tells us that the kings "took all the goods of Sodom and Gomorrah and all their food and went on." The kings would also kidnap Lot who was living in Sodom, taking his possessions as well.

Who was told of this kidnapping? Abram. After assembling 318 "trained men," he and his men pursued the kings and their men, going "as far as Hobah to the north of Damascus." When it was over, Abram had rescued Lot and his goods, "as well as the women and the other people" (see Genesis 14:15–16).

Ten years later, in the land of Canaan, Sarai would give her Egyptian handmaiden, Hagar, to Abram to take as his wife. Sarai was upset she hadn't been able to have any children. So instead of waiting on God to fulfill His covenant with Abram (see Genesis 15:5; 17:6–8), Sarai would propose that Abram take Hagar as his own and father a child through her. There is much to be said about waiting (see "Just Wait Awhile" diagram).

Such a relationship between Abram and Hagar would occur (see Genesis 16:3). It was a contentious relationship between Sarai and Hagar. After running away, an angel of the *Lord* would approach Hagar telling her that she would give birth to a son, and his name would be Ishmael. Genesis 16:16 tells us that Abram was eighty-six years old when Ishmael was born.

Nearly fourteen years later, when Abram was ninety-nine years old, God appeared before him. How exciting it must have been for Abram for God to have come to him. There was much good news for God to deliver:

"I will establish My covenant between Me and you, and I will multiply you greatly" (Genesis 17:2).

"As for Me, My covenant is with you: you will become the father of many nations" (Genesis 17:4).

"Your name will no longer be Abram, but your name will be Abraham for I will make you the father of many nations" (Genesis 17:5).

The name Abraham is thought to mean "father of a multitude." God would also change Sarai's name to Sarah which means "princess."

In Genesis 17:9, God tells Abraham, "As for you, you and your offspring after you throughout their generations are to keep My covenant." (As noted earlier, God spoke about the Abrahamic Covenant in Genesis 12:1–3 and 15:18–21.) He would, in Genesis 17:16, tell Abraham that "I will bless her; indeed, I will give you a son by her. I will bless her, and she will produce nations; kings of peoples will come from her." Abraham questioned this proclamation wondering out loud if a child can be born to a man who would be one hundred years old at the birth of the infant. However, age would not deter God from such a blessing. He would go on to tell Abraham in Genesis 17:19, "Your wife Sarah will bear you a son, and you will name him Isaac."

Although God would state later in Genesis 17:20 that He would "certainly bless [Ishmael]" making "him fruitful and [multiplying] greatly," God told Abraham in Genesis 17:19 that "I will confirm My covenant with him [Isaac] as an everlasting covenant for his future offspring."

Visitors to the Camp

After God's visit with Abraham, the men in Abraham's camp would obey God's command. Sometime thereafter, three men would appear suddenly in the sight of Abraham as he sat at the entrance to his tent. As was custom during those days, Abraham ran down to the visitors, greeting them and bowing down "to the ground" (see Genesis 18:2). As Swindoll puts it, such a bow would indicate that Abraham knew there was "something special about these visitors." He called one of the men "My lord" (Genesis 18:1 begins by saying that "then the *Lord* appeared") suggesting that this was the preincarnate Christ. Abraham invited the three men to stay for a while to rest and eat.

Upon agreeing, Abraham and Sarah personally prepared a meal for the men. When Abraham took the food to where the men were under one of the oaks of Mamre they asked him where Sarah was.

> "Then he said, 'Let the Lord not be angry, and I will speak one more time. Suppose 10 are found there?'" (Genesis 18:32)

He replied that she was in their tent nearby. We are told in Genesis 18:10 that "the *Lord* said, 'I will certainly come back to you in about a year's time, and your wife Sarah will have a son!'" Sarah overheard this and laughed, thinking she was too old. The Lord heard her laugh and wondered why she thought she was too old to have a baby. He pointed out that all things are possible with the Lord. Sarah would deny laughing, but the Lord heard her. We are never too old to be used by the Lord for His purposes.

Afterward, the Lord would tell Abraham in Genesis 18:20 about the concern regarding Sodom and Gomorrah saying that "their sin is extremely serious." Abraham became very concerned. After two of the men went toward Sodom, the *Lord* and Abraham would talk about the imminent plans for the city. The Lord is omniscient He knows about future events long before they happen. From where they stood on the mountainside, they had a good view of Sodom. Abraham, who had a caring heart, asked the Lord in Genesis 18:23, "Will You really sweep away the righteous with the wicked?" He knows about future events long before they happen. He then injects several what if scenarios over the next several verses: "What if there are 50 righteous people in the city? Will you destroy the whole city for lack of five [meaning 45]? Suppose 30 are found there?" He would question the Lord's intent to bring destruction to Sodom if there were just ten righteous people.

With each question, the Lord responded that if it were so, He would not destroy the city.

Sodom and Gomorrah

We read that Lot is at the gate of Sodom. He is working with the elders who are ruling the city. Being at the gate to determine who gets in is an important role. When the two men (angels) who visited with Abraham came up to the gate that night, Lot encourages them

Here are Swindoll's five principles from Abram's display of unfaithfulness:

1. *Everyone* faces famines in their lives.
2. Every escape contains a lie (i.e., "I can handle this without the Lord).
3. Every Abram struggles with a *weakness*. We're all weak, and we need supernatural help.
4. Every compromise jeopardizes a Sarai. There's no such thing as a victimless sin, including the sins you keep private.
5. Every Egypt has a Pharaoh. We live among people *who do not know our God.* When they see us blindly blundering through life making unwise or sinful choices, we bring shame to God rather than glory.

to spend the night at his home, and then they can be on their way the following morning. The men's intent was to visit and sleep in the square so that they would have insight into the sins occurring in Sodom. However, Lot would not have that. Part of providing hospitality to visitors was protecting them. He was determined to do so regardless of the situation.

When Lot brought the men into his house, such action did not go unnoticed by the men of Sodom. They would surround the house demanding that Lot send the two men out. He refused, offering his daughters instead. When the crowd tried to get in, Genesis 19:10 tells us, "But the angels reached out, brought Lot into the house with them, and shut the door." The men who tried to get into Lot's house were then struck with a blinding light that prevented them from finding the house's entrance.

The angels then told Lot to gather up his family and get out of the city. In Genesis 19:13, the angels told them why: "For we are about to destroy this place because the outcry against its people is so great before the *Lord*, that the *Lord* has sent us to destroy it." Early the following morning, Lot, his wife, and their two daughters obeyed, escaping the atrocities of Sodom. In so doing, the angels told them not to look back. Sodom and Gomorrah were destroyed. During the destruction, Lot's wife did look back and was turned into a pillar of salt.

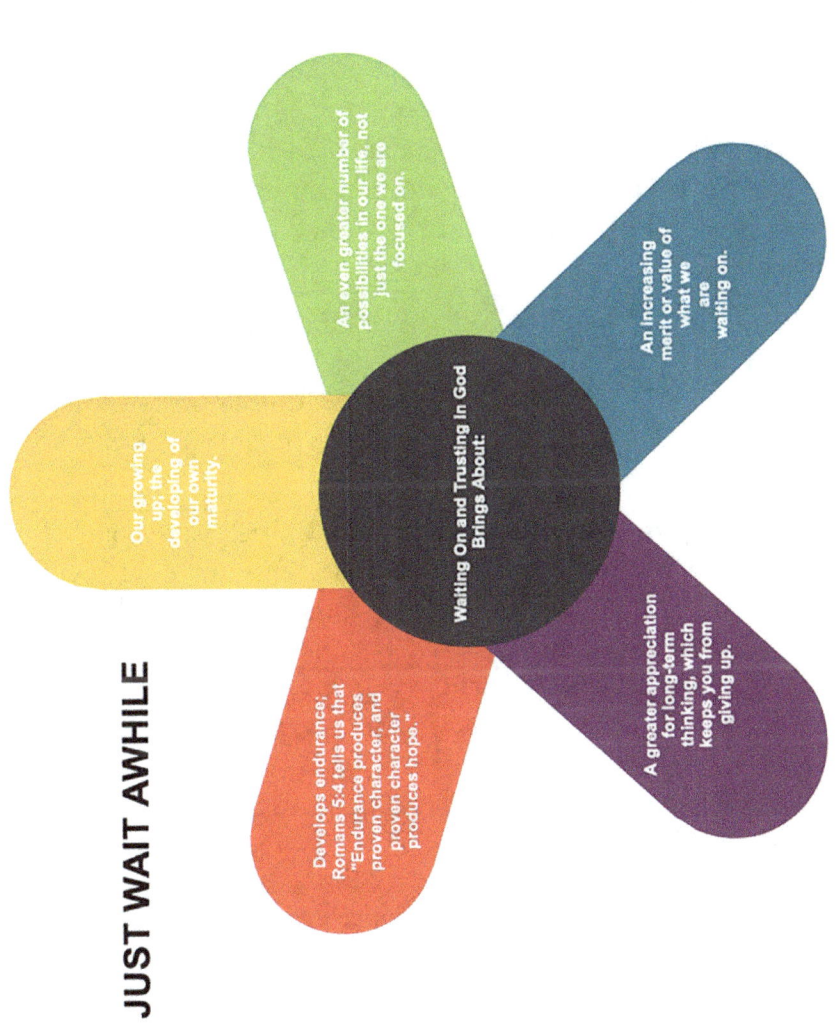

JUST WAIT AWHILE

An even greater number of possibilities in our life, not just the one we are focused on.

An increasing merit or value of what we are waiting on.

Our growing up; the developing of our own maturity.

Waiting On and Trusting In God Brings About:

Develops endurance; Romans 5:4 tells us that "Endurance produces proven character, and proven character produces hope."

A greater appreciation for long-term thinking, which keeps you from giving up.

A Son Comes to Abraham and Sarah

As God had promised, Sarah became pregnant and would deliver a son "to Abraham in his old age, at the appointed time God had told him" (see Genesis 21:2). Abraham named their son Isaac.

There would eventually be contention between Ishmael and Isaac. Having seen enough of it, Sarah demanded that Abraham send Ishmael and Hagar away. "Drive out this slave with her son, for the son of this slave will not be a coheir with my son Isaac" (Genesis 21:10)! After being told by God to do as Sarah had said, Abraham obeyed sending Hagar and Ishmael on their way.

God would test Abraham spiritually in Genesis 22. In verse 2, God told Abraham to "take your son, your only son Isaac, whom you love, go to the land of Moriah and offer him there as a burnt offering on one of the mountains I will tell you about." This would be a difficult thing to do as a parent. But it was God directing Abraham a man who had faith in God, trusting Him completely. His heart was right with God.

> "And Abraham named that place The *Lord* Will Provide, so today it is said, 'It will be provided on the Lord's mountain'" (Genesis 22:14).

After traveling to Moriah and preparing the boy for the sacrifice, angel would intervene, saying to Abraham, "Do not lay a hand on the boy or do anything to him. For now I know that you fear God, since you have not withheld your only son from Me" (see Genesis 22:12). Looking around, Abraham noticed a ram whose horns were caught in the thicket. The ram would be used as a sacrifice in place of Abraham's son.

> "Wait for the *Lord*; be strong and courageous. Wait for the *Lord*" (Psalm 27:14)

Sarah would live 127 years. Upon her death in Hebron, Abraham was given what was considered the best burial place in which he could bury Sarah. He would die at the age of 175 and be buried alongside his wife, Sarah.

Isaac The Child of the Covenant

Isaac is considered by some to be the miracle child. Why is this? Because his parents, Abraham and Sarah, were childless until much later in life. In fact, as we read in the previous chapter on Abraham, Sarah laughed when she heard that she was going to have a son. However, God is faithful and, at ninety years old, Sarah would give birth to a son. Isaac was born in 1896 BC and died in 1716 BC.

How important a role does Isaac play besides being the son to Abraham and Sarah (hint: God's covenant to Abraham)? In Genesis 21:12, God tells Abraham to listen to his wife Sarah when she previously said in verse 10 to "drive out this slave with her son, for the son of this slave will not be a coheir with my son Isaac!" God also told Abraham something very important: "Your offspring will be traced through Isaac."

It wasn't easy for Abraham to do because, after all, Ishmael was his son. However, Abraham would send Ishmael and his mother, Hagar, away with food and water. Later on, Abraham would be tested with a bigger trial a spiritual test. Abraham would be told by God to take Isaac to the land of Moriah and "offer him there as a burnt offering on one of the mountains I will tell you about" (see Genesis 22:2).

How old was Isaac at this time? There is no consensus among theologians and scholars as to the age of Isaac when Abraham brought him up to the mountain to be sacrificed. He is considered by most to have been a young man. After preparing Isaac for sacrifice, preparing him to be killed on Mount Moriah, an Angel of the *Lord* intervened. "Do not lay a hand on the boy or do anything to him" (see Genesis 22:12). Who was this Angel of the *Lord*? (Hint: He goes on to say in verse 12, "For now I know that you fear God, since you have not withheld your only son from Me.") Look at the last word in this sentence Me. If you said God, you are right! Afterward, Abraham noticed a ram caught in some briar. He would offer it to God as a burnt offering in place of Isaac.

Here are the takeaways from this incident:

1. Abraham's faith and confidence in the Lord. He showed his faith in the Lord by doing something most parents would find impossible of doing. Think about how long Abraham and Sarah had to wait to have a child of their own! Abraham loved his son, Isaac. Now, he's being told by the Lord to sacrifice him! Did Abraham question Him? Early on, Abraham (and Sarah) made decisions that didn't take into account God's will. Did such total faith in the Lord take hold prior to preparing Isaac for sacrifice? God had been leading him during this journey from his hometown of Ur. God had been showing His love and faithfulness along the journey. Abraham's trust in the Lord grew. I think many of us can relate to Ray Stedman's statement: "Here was a man who was far from perfect, yet who lived by faith." None of us are perfect, but not all of us live by faith in the Lord Jesus Christ. Are we willing to make the sacrifices to achieve His will? Abraham was. From Genesis 12–22, we read about Abraham maturing in his faith, depending on God's promises, and with patience realizing that God is faithful and indeed loving.

2. Isaac's confidence exuded toward his father; his consent to be a sacrifice to the Lord also showed his faith in the Lord. He willingly laid himself down on the woodpile to be a burnt offering. This showing of faith in God on the part of a father is a prelude to the greatest story ever told: God offering "His only begotten Son" on the same mountain on which Isaac was going to be sacrificed on.

Isaac loved his mother, Sarah. He was deeply saddened when she died. She was 127 years old. For three years, he would grieve for his mother. God would choose Rebekah to be Isaac's wife (see Genesis 24:14). Soon thereafter, Isaac would marry Rebekah (see Genesis 24:67). Rebekah filled the emptiness in Isaac's heart created by his mother's death. She would replace Sarah as the *matriarch, or head, of the family.*

Like his parents, Isaac and Rebekah went for a period of time before giving birth to twins both boys.

Upon the death of his father, Abraham, Isaac would now be the patriarch of the family.

WHO WAS ISAAC?

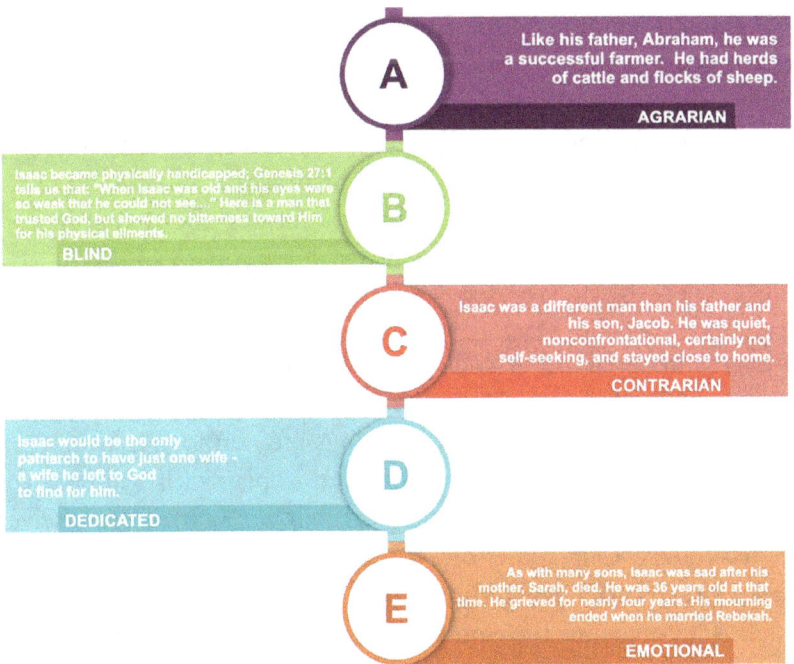

A — Like his father, Abraham, he was a successful farmer. He had herds of cattle and flocks of sheep. **AGRARIAN**

B — Isaac became physically handicapped; Genesis 27:1 tells us that: "When Isaac was old and his eyes were so weak that he could not see..." Here is a man that trusted God, but showed no bitterness toward Him for his physical ailments. **BLIND**

C — Isaac was a different man than his father and his son, Jacob. He was quiet, nonconfrontational, certainly not self-seeking, and stayed close to home. **CONTRARIAN**

D — Isaac would be the only patriarch to have just one wife - a wife he left to God to find for him. **DEDICATED**

E — As with many sons, Isaac was sad after his mother, Sarah, died. He was 36 years old at that time. He grieved for nearly four years. His mourning ended when he married Rebekah. **EMOTIONAL**

But I will confirm My covenant with Isaac.

Genesis 17:21

Jacob The Second Son
Who Became First

---✦---

Two nations are in your womb; two people will come from you and be separated. One people will be stronger than the other, and the older will serve the younger.

-Genesis 25:23

How many of you are twins? Those of you that are, how many of you were born first? How many of you think you and your twin sibling fought inside your mother's womb? I'm a twin and was born first. If you're competitive, this can be a trophy-awarded kind of event. I speak up when asked who was the firstborn. I tell whoever wants to know that I was born twenty-four minutes ahead of my sister. However, in this day and age, it really doesn't matter, does it, as to who is born first or last? I mean, it's not like the days of Isaac and

What is a material thing? Well, it's a toy, a book, an electronic gadget, a video game, clothing, etc. As you get older, it may be a car, a house, shoes, and more. However, these things are temporary. Your shoes will eventually wear out; a toy you loved to play with will bore you one day. The excitement of a new car will wear off. We, ourselves, are temporary. Our bodies one day will wear out. *But* knowing and trusting the Lord, having Him in your heart, and helping others as a result is permanent. The Apostle Paul tells us in 2 Corinthians 4:18, "So we do not focus on what is seen, but on what is unseen. For what is seen is temporary, but what is unseen is eternal."

Rebekah who were blessed with twin sons. After all, back then, there was a birthright given to the firstborn along with a blessing.

How many of you know the names of the two boys born to Isaac and Rebekah? If you guessed Esau and Jacob, you were right! Esau was born first. He had a head full of hair, red at that! He was a tough person, growing up liking to hunt and fish. He just loved the outdoors. Jacob, on the other hand, was more quiet and liked being close to home. He became a good farmer and tended to the sheep like his grandfather (Abraham) and his dad.

Every child is different, which should be okay with the parents. No parent should show favoritism toward a child; however, both Isaac and Rebekah did. Isaac favored Esau for his love of hunting and would bring his father wild game he caught. Isaac loved it when Esau did this. Rebekah, on the other hand, favored Jacob because he was helpful in taking care of the home and showed how much he loved his mother.

Have you ever been so hungry you couldn't stand it? You'd see something you were craving for and you just had to have it no matter the cost. Well, Esau came in from hunting one day. He was absolutely starving! He smelled the delicious stew that Jacob was cooking, and he just had to have some! Jacob, somewhat conniving, knew how hungry his brother was. It was a perfect time to get the birthright from Esau. And he did! Just like that! Esau agreed to trade his birthright for some food because he thought he was going to die if he didn't eat!

Was this right for Jacob to connive to get Esau's birthright? If you wanted something so bad, would you do as Jacob did? Do you think God was surprised by Jacob's action? Simply, no. First (and always remember this), God is omniscient. He knows everything. He knows what you and I are going to do long before we do it. He knew Esau was not worthy of having the birthright before the twins were born! Esau was caught up in material things. He liked worldly stuff.

Of even greater concern was that Esau wasn't a spiritual person. Ask yourself this where does one, such as Esau, who is into having nice things place God in his life? To what do the scales tip to?

Soon, Jacob (with the help of his mother Rebekah) would also get the blessing from Isaac, his father. Should we connive our way, like they did, into getting something we want? God had told both Isaac and Rebekah that He would give Jacob the covenant blessing before the twins were born. Yet, like you and me, they thought they knew better. Sometimes, we get impatient, or we like to control things thinking we know better than anyone including God! However, there are always lessons to be learned. God is in control, and He has the final say.

Lessons to Be Learned

A few things happened after Jacob and Rebekah's scheme landed him the blessing what Esau thought was *his* blessing from Isaac. Was there rejoicing? No. Instead of waiting on the Lord to take action, the conniving brought on by favoritism didn't bring the joy and pleasure that Jacob and his mother must have thought would come. Esau was angry. Oh, he was very angry. Isaac wasn't too happy either that he had been manipulated. Jacob and Rebekah both feared for the safety of Jacob's life.

If they had lived in the time of David, maybe he could have talked some sense into Jacob and Rebekah. David would have told them, "Wait for the *Lord*; be strong and courageous. Wait for the *Lord*" (Psalm 27:14). King David is expressing the confidence and faith he has in the Lord. He doesn't fear as he knows the Lord is his light and salvation. Knowing this, believing in the Lord and His faithfulness would have kept Jacob and his mother from taking it upon themselves to secure the birthright and blessing that God was going to give to Jacob anyway.

A mother now has to protect a son whom she put in harm's way. Rebekah would now send Jacob to Haran to live with his uncle Laban, fearing that Esau would kill him. Aren't we like that at some point in our lives? We make rash decisions then worry about the consequences. So off went Jacob down the road a homebody and now a traveling man! One night during his journey, Jacob dreamt about a ladder that stretched from heaven to earth. Going up and down this ladder were God's angels. Above the ladder stood God. In the dream, God passed down the covenant He made with Abraham to Jacob. Have you ever been afraid of your parents? Well, Jacob became afraid of God to the point of revering Him. God uses dreams throughout the Bible to speak to us, revealing His plan, giving us foresight to protect that which He has laid out.

Upon reaching the land owned by Laban, Jacob had his first encounter with his future wife, Rachel, who will be the mother later on of two of his children, Joseph and Benjamin. Upon learning that Jacob was her father's nephew, Rachel hurriedly ran back to tell her father. Laban embraced Jacob, telling Jacob that he could stay and work for him. Upon asking how much his wages "should be," Jacob expressed his love for Rachel, stating that he would

Esau's *birthright* was the right to be recognized as the firstborn. It carried with it a lot of responsibility as well as financial gain. The birthright meant that Esau would receive a double portion of the inheritance from Isaac. There would also be a ceremonial blessing from Isaac. Such a blessing carried with it a special relationship with God.

However, God had already told Isaac and Rebekah that "the older will serve the younger." We need to listen to God when He speaks to us.

work for seven years for her hand in marriage. Laban agreed but tricked Jacob into marrying his firstborn daughter, Leah. The deceit played by Jacob earlier to get the blessing from his father, Isaac, had now come back around to Jacob who was deceived by Rachel's father. Although upset, Jacob agreed to work another seven years in order to marry Rachel whom he truly loved. Although having more than one spouse at a time is illegal today in the United States, it was not the case thousands of years before the birth of Jesus Christ.

Jacob would father twelve sons and one daughter to four different women including Leah and Rachel. Upon the direction of the Lord, Jacob decided it was time to return home. After smoothing over issues with Laban, the two men agreed to separate peaceably (see Genesis 31). Jacob, who became very wealthy during his stay, took his families back home to Bethel.

But he wanted to make peace with Esau. He wasn't sure what to expect from his brother other than he knew at one time his brother wanted to kill him as an act of revenge for Jacob's deceit. He was told that Esau was coming to him with four hundred men. Upon hearing this, did Jacob turn toward God, remembering his dream years earlier of God's angelic army? No, he took matters into his own hands, dividing his group of people into two camps. He then prayed out of fear to "God of my father Abraham and God of my father Isaac." We can try to do things ourselves, but in the end, we need the Lord.

That night, Jacob would set aside a certain number of the things he and his family were bringing back as gifts to Esau. Jacob's conscience had been bothering him all this time and hoped that these gifts would appease Esau. After sending his servants on ahead to deliver the gifts, including animals, to his brother, Jacob would have another encounter. This is like a child who continues to disobey his or her parents. Eventually, one or both of the parents have to have a one-on-one meeting with the child. God was going to do just that, encountering Jacob on a mountaintop. He would change Jacob's name (which meant "to deceive") to Israel (which means "he struggled with God"). God would also dislocate Jacob's hip causing him to permanently limp as a reminder of his encounter with God.

That morning, Jacob and Esau would reunite as brothers, not enemies. Jacob and his family would then settle down in Shechem, in the land of Canaan.

Joseph A Brother Betrayed

✦

Do you come from a large family? Do you have brothers and/or sisters? Do you sometimes have to get everyone's attention with a story of something that happened to you like winning the spelling bee or having the best science project? I'm sure you excel in some event, and your parent(s) are proud of you. One last thing, in taking first place at something, have your brothers and/or sisters given you a high five or a frown face? The following story is about a boy, Joseph, who had to deal with jealous brothers, conniving brothers at that!

The Bible begins the story of Joseph in Genesis 37. He is seventeen years old at this time. Second youngest of the twelve boys, he is the favorite of his father, Israel. He was given a coat of multicolor from Israel as a sign of the love that he had for Joseph. Now it does seem strange that Israel would show favoritism to one of his sons since he had to endure favoritism that his father, Isaac, showed toward his brother Esau. Nevertheless, Israel was very fond of his son Joseph and his brothers knew it and didn't like it.

One day, Joseph told his brothers of a dream he had in which "my sheaf stood up, and your sheaves gathered around it and bowed down to my sheaf" (Genesis 37:7). His brothers didn't take too kindly to this dream. They voiced their opinion that Joseph would not rule over them and that they wouldn't be bowing down to him. But the dreams wouldn't stop.

He had another dream in which "the sun, moon, and 11 stars were bowing down to me" (Genesis 37:9). After telling his brothers of this dream, they became more bitter toward him. Even his father criticized Joseph sharply. As a result, Joseph sharing this dream made things even more difficult at home.

One day, Israel asked Joseph to check on his brothers who were taking care of the family's flocks in Shechem. Upon entering Shechem, he began looking for his brothers, wandering in a field in which he thought they would be. A man passing by asked him who he was looking for. When Joseph mentioned his brothers and their flock, the man immediately told him he overhead them say they were going to go to Dothan.

Getting to Dothan, Joseph spotted his brothers. They saw him as well. It was here that they plotted to get rid of their little brother. All but one, Reuben, wanted to kill Joseph. Reuben instead wanted them to throw their brother into a pit. He had planned to return later to rescue him.

Stripping him of his multicolored robe, Joseph's brothers threw him into the dry empty pit. They called him a "dreamer." When a caravan of Ishmaelites got closer, the brothers decided not to harm Joseph but to sell him to these people. For twenty pieces of silver, the Midianites took Joseph as their slave and headed to Egypt. Unaware of his brothers' action, Reuben returned to the pit and was startled to find it empty. After learning what his brothers did, they devised a story to take the blame off of them. They would tear up the robe, soak it in goat's blood, and make it look to their father, Israel, that Joseph had been killed by a wild animal. Israel was devastated thinking he had lost forever his beloved son Joseph. At this point, out of nothing but jealousy, they had gotten rid of their brother Joseph and had lied to their father as to what happened to him.

Meanwhile, the Midianites arrived in Egypt. Finding Potiphar, who was the captain of the guard and an officer to Pharaoh, they arranged to sell Joseph to him. After being sold, Joseph found himself working in Potiphar's home. Although no doubt saddened by what his brothers had done, he would become successful under Potiphar. Potiphar put him in charge of his household. The Lord was with Joseph.

Unfortunately, Potiphar's wife wanted Joseph. One day, when the workers weren't at home, she tried again to get Joseph's attention. He refused and ran away. However, in his attempt to quickly escape, he forgot to get his cloak that she had grabbed off of him. Angry, she then lied to her servants and then to her husband telling them, with the cloak in one hand, that Joseph had sought her out. She lied. Potiphar threw him in jail. The Lord was with Joseph, however.

In jail, the warden showed favor to Joseph putting him in charge of all the prisoners in the jail. The warden trusted Joseph with everything that went on at the jail. The Lord hadn't left Joseph. He continued to help Joseph be successful. We, who believe in the Lord, are never alone. He walks with us when we are at our peaks and in the valleys of our lives.

While Joseph was in jail, Pharaoh had both his cupbearer and baker thrown into jail the very jail that housed Joseph. They were both assigned to Joseph. Joseph was their personal attendant. Notice the constant responsibility given to Joseph. One night, the cupbearer and the baker each had a dream. They weren't sure what these dreams meant. Have you ever had a dream that when you awoke, you wondered what was behind the dream? Well, this was the case with both men. The next morning, Joseph heard their dreams and helped them with their meanings. Joseph had good news for the cupbearer: he would be restored to his position under Pharaoh. In return for the good news, Joseph asked the cupbearer to tell Pharaoh about him. The baker, thinking that Joseph would give him the same positive news, was stunned when Joseph said that his dream meant he would be executed in three days. Indeed, Pharaoh returned the cupbearer to his former position. The baker, however, was hung. Unfortunately for Joseph, the cupbearer forgot to tell Pharaoh about Joseph.

Two years later, Pharaoh had two dreams that disturbed him. When morning came, he summoned several who could help interpret what his dreams meant. He scurried about, summoning all the country's wise men and magicians. They had no answers for Pharaoh's dreams! But one person under Pharaoh did the cupbearer! He had forgotten about Joseph and his correct interpretation of the cupbearer's and baker's dreams. Feeling sad that he had forgotten to tell Pharaoh earlier about Joseph, he mentioned Joseph to the Pharaoh. He told him Joseph would be able to tell Pharaoh exactly what his two dreams meant! Pharaoh sent for Joseph!

When he went before Pharaoh, Joseph told him that it wasn't he but God who will interpret Pharaoh's dreams. Pharaoh went ahead and explained the dreams to Joseph. The first dream included healthy cows and sickly ones. The second dream consisted of beautifully grown stalks of grain followed by thin dried-up stalks of grain. After hearing the dreams, Joseph told him that God was showing Pharaoh what He was soon going to do! This is what Joseph told Pharaoh:

"Seven years of great abundance are coming throughout the land of Egypt. After them, seven years of famine will take place and all the land of Egypt will be forgotten. The famine will devastate the land" (Genesis 41:29–30).

Joseph went on to tell Pharaoh that having two dreams that meant the same was God's way of saying that the events were going to happen soon. Joseph encouraged Pharaoh to look for a wise man who would successfully lead them through this period of abundance then famine. He proposed the storage of grain during the years of abundance then having it available during the years of famine. Pharaoh liked Joseph's suggestions so much so that he looked to him and said, "Since God has made all this known to you, there is no one as intelligent and wise as you are" (Genesis 41:39). Pharaoh would not only choose Joseph to lead Egypt through the upcoming years of abundance and famine but also made him second in command. Only Pharaoh would be greater than Joseph. God was with Joseph.

Accepting the responsibility, Joseph would successfully lead Egypt through both the good and difficult times. As a result of his leadership, other countries also impacted by the famine came to Joseph requesting to buy grain for their people. Others that came to buy grain from Egypt were the sons of Israel. When they stepped in front of Joseph to buy grain, they did not recognize him, but he recognized his brothers (Israel did not allow Benjamin to go with them to Egypt as he was now his favored son and didn't want to lose him). After bowing to Joseph, he accused them of being spies. Denying this did them no good as Joseph had them imprisoned for three days. On the third day, Joseph told them he was going to hold one of them (Simeon) while the rest would take bags of grain back to their households. They were then to bring back their youngest brother. They agreed to do so; however, on the way back, one of the brothers opened his sack and found not just grain but the money he had brought to buy the grain. Later on, they all emptied their sacks and came across their original bags of money.

Jacob, upset with the current circumstances and not wanting anything to happen to Benjamin, refused for his sons to take him back to Egypt. However, after hearing Judah (Jacob's fourth oldest son) assured the safety of Benjamin, Israel relented. He sent his sons back to Joseph with an impressive gift along with twice the amount of money that they originally had. Israel told them to return the money for the grain Joseph had earlier given them.

Upon return, Joseph's steward acknowledged that he had received their money. In return, he brought Simeon out to his brothers. He also gave them water to wash their feet and fed their donkeys. At noon, they sat down for lunch with Joseph bringing the gift that Jacob had given them to give Joseph. Upon seeing Benjamin, Joseph hurriedly ran to another room and wept. After gaining composure, he returned to the eating area. The Bible tells us that since Egyptians didn't eat with Hebrews, the brothers sat at a different table. Everyone enjoyed the meal. Later, Joseph would have his steward fill his brothers' bags with a lot of food and the money they brought back to him. Then, upon being ordered, the steward placed a silver cup in the bag that belonged to Benjamin. After the brothers left the following morning, Joseph had his steward chase them down. Upon inspecting the bags, the steward came across the cup in Benjamin's bag. His brothers were aghast! How could this have happened? Upon return to Joseph's house, they pleaded to bring Benjamin back with them, for they knew if he didn't return, Israel would surely die. He loved Benjamin. Joseph had seen and heard enough. After becoming emotional, he ordered everyone out of the room except his brothers. It was here that he told them he was Joseph the brother they sold into slavery years ago. They embraced each other.

Joseph had his father Israel, along with all his possessions, brought to Egypt from the land of Canaan transported via wagons supplied by Pharaoh. God would eventually bring His people back to their land, the Promised Land, faithfully keeping the covenant He made with Abraham.

Joseph His Character and Forgiveness
"God Planned It for Good"

How many of you have said one of the following:

- ☐ It's tough to be in school today.
- ☐ It's tough to make friends.
- ☐ People are so mean.
- ☐ He/she did that to me.
- ☐ No one listens to me.

The Character of Joseph

Life is not easy. I hate to be the bearer of bad news, but nowhere in the Bible are we guaranteed a happy or an easy life. No one knows this better than Joseph. His early years, all the way through young adulthood, were hard. He had eleven brothers to deal with. He was the second youngest of the boys. With the exception of Benjamin, the other boys were his half brothers. At one time, there were four mothers in the household: Rachel, Leah, Bilhah, and Zilpah. It was a house divided for sure.

There was a lot for Joseph to handle. On top of everything else, his mother, Rachel, died in childbirth when he was in his mid-teens. Can you imagine the emotions he went through as a result? He is then thrust into being a spy for his father Jacob, who suspected his older sons of some misdeed while tending sheep. We don't know what Joseph's feelings were in being asked to rat on his brothers. But he respected his father, Jacob, who seemed to really love his boy. Joseph would report back to Jacob on things he saw. We don't know what the consequences were, but when you read Genesis 37, you get the feeling that Joseph's brothers were punished in some way. The brothers sought revenge, which is never the answer, then and now.

CHARACTER

Joseph, the son of patriarch Jacob, is such a perfect example of the need to persevere even when times are tough. The apostle Paul tells us in Romans 5:3-4 "[3]And not only that, but we also rejoice in our afflictions, because we know that affliction produces endurance, [4] produces proven character, and proven character produces hope." Joseph proved his character, enduring hardships, yet standing firm with God's will.

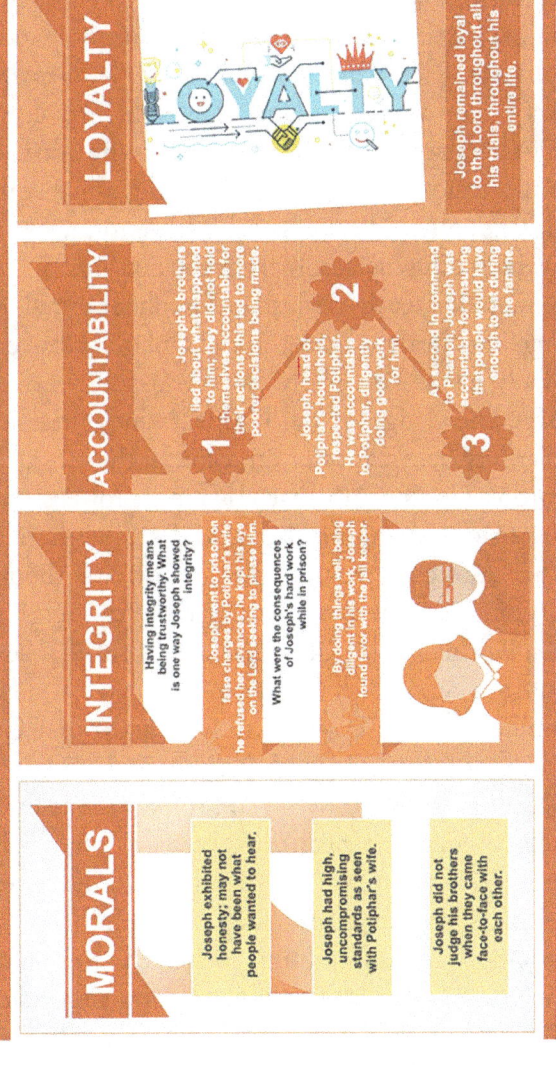

MORALS

Joseph exhibited honesty; may not have been what people wanted to hear.

Joseph had high, uncompromising standards as seen with Potiphar's wife.

Joseph did not judge his brothers when they came face-to-face with each other.

INTEGRITY

Having integrity means being trustworthy. What is one way Joseph showed integrity?

Joseph went to prison on false charges by Potiphar's wife; he refused her advances; he kept his eyes on the Lord seeking to please Him.

What were the consequences of Joseph's hard work while in prison?

By doing things well, being diligent in his work, Joseph found favor with the jail keeper.

ACCOUNTABILITY

1 Joseph's brothers lied about what happened to him; they did not hold themselves accountable for their actions; this led to more poorer decisions being made.

2 Joseph, head of Potiphar's household, respected Potiphar. He was accountable to Potiphar, diligently doing good work for him.

3 As second in command to Pharaoh, Joseph was accountable for ensuring that people would have enough to eat during the famine.

LOYALTY

Joseph remained loyal to the Lord throughout all his trials, throughout his entire life.

The Character of Joseph

Joseph perhaps wasn't aware or didn't want to believe that there was any meanness or jealously toward him by his own family. In his heart, he was focused on the Lord. Jacob had undoubtedly told his sons about the greatness of the Lord. Such talks appeared to have stuck with Joseph. Through all the trials he would go through, Joseph kept his eyes on God discerning that there was a purpose God had for the trials of Joseph's life. Rick Warren, in his book *The Purpose Driven Life,* puts it this way: "you were made for a mission." Joseph was. Knowing this later on in life, having put the pieces of his life's puzzle together, Joseph forgave those along the path of his young adult years. We see that in the end, through God's plans and intervention, Joseph saved the lives of many, including his family from the famine.

Remember, each trial that Joseph endured had a reason for occurring. His heart was in the right place. How else could he have coped with it all. For nearly two thousand years, we have had the wonderful knowledge of the Gospel, which Joseph didn't have. We know that forgiveness for our sins came at the cross. Christ died for our sins He took God's wrath that was meant for each of us; He defeated death by rising on the third day, and sits at the right hand of God the Father Almighty. For Joseph, almost two thousand years before the birth of Christ, he was able to see the sovereignty of God at work at each milestone in his life. God is faithful in His promises, in His covenant that began with Abraham, then Isaac, followed by Jacob. The Abrahamic Covenant is a depiction of grace that God extended to a people He sought to have a relationship with.

We all go through tough times. No one is immune from issues or difficulties that can take the air out of one's balloon. When you have a tough day, think of Joseph and his trials. Joseph, however, was never alone. God was at his side the whole time. He realized at the end that God is faithful to bring good even to the most difficult trying times. It's easy to wonder why God is putting us through a certain pain. What God seeks is that you will have that continual hope as you hurdle difficult periods in your life. Although Paul would write this a few thousand years after Joseph, he and Joseph would be in agreement with Romans 5:3–4: "And not only that, but we also rejoice in our afflictions, because we know that affliction produces endurance, endurance produces proven character, and proven character produces hope." The Bible gives us insight into the lives of others that came way before but whose lives were no different than ours. Oh yes, the environment was different, the settings more primitive. However, there was one entity then as there is now, thousands of years later, who continues to show His love for us: God. He didn't desert Noah, Abraham, Isaac, Jacob, or Joseph, and He won't desert you.

"You planned evil against me; God planned it for good to bring about the present result the survival of many people" (Genesis 50:20).

References

Cumming, Greg. "The Terebinth Tree of Moreh." Good News for Israel, www.goodnewsforisrael.com/2018/06/15/20-the-terebinth-tree-of-moreh/. Accessed 2 August 2020.

Ham, Ken. 2014. *The New Answers Book 4*. Master Books. Hodge, Bodie. 2014. *Tower of Babel*. Master Books.

Hunter, Margaret. "Melchizedek and Shem." Amazing Bible Timeline, www.amazingbibletimeline.com/blog/melchizedek-and-shem/. Accessed 5 May 2020.

MacArthur, John. 2017. T*he Gospel According to Paul*. Thomas Nelson.

McManus, Erwin Raphael. 2006. *Soul Cravings*. Thomas Nelson.

Swindoll, Chuck. 2014. *Abraham*. Tyndale House Publishers, Inc.

Taylor, Paul F. "Noah the Evangelist." Answers in Genesis,

About the Author

✦

Alda Stephens has been, for twelve years, a Sunday school teacher in the children's ministry at First Baptist Church Woodstock (FBCW), a twenty-thousand-plus member megachurch located in Woodstock, Georgia. In addition to teaching, Ms. Stephens has been a leader in FBCW's LoveLoud program that has served as an outreach in meeting the needs of the surrounding communities. She has also volunteered her time for a number of years with the FBCW Vacation Bible School program.

A degreed engineer, Ms. Stephens served on Southern Polytechnic State University's alumni association board (now part of Kennesaw State University) in various capacities including president for two years. She is the founder of The Outtop an online educational site devoted to teaching God's Word as well as that of US history, politics, and business.

She lives in Canton, Georgia, with her husband. They have two adult children and a grandchild.

www.ingramcontent.com/pod-product-compliance
Lightning Source LLC
Chambersburg PA
CBHW060353130626
46553CB00003B/1204